Hidden
In His
Hands

Hidden In His Hands

Basilea Schlink

Bethany Fellowship INC.
MINNEAPOLIS, MINNESOTA 55438

Published in England by
Marshall, Morgan & Scott

Hidden in His Hands
Basilea Schlink

Library of Congress Catalog Card Number 79-52346

ISBN 0-87123-208-1

Published by Bethany Fellowship, Inc.
6820 Auto Club Road, Minneapolis, Minnesota 55438

Printed in the United States of America

Table of Contents

Basilea Schlink has written over 100 titles with translations in more than 30 languages. Her work has been acclaimed by Christian leaders throughout the world, and her inspired writings on a large variety of subjects have been a source of blessing to many.

When all else fails us, there is Someone who will never fail us — our heavenly Father. The great Creator of the universe cares for each one of us personally. The very hairs on our head are numbered. Nothing escapes His loving eye; nothing is too far removed from His reach. And in His hands we are sheltered from the raging storm.

HIDDEN IN HIS HANDS — an encouraging selection of spiritual devotions! As we read this book, we shall discover how to experience security in God, and this will return to us as a source of strength and comfort in times of hardship.

Jesus Christ says,

*In the world
you have tribulation;
but be of good cheer,
I have overcome
the world.*

John 16:33

Hidden in His Hands

Darkness covers the nations today. All humanity is imperilled to an unprecedented extent. A sense of insecurity, a fear of uprisings, violence, disasters and of a nuclear war govern the majority of people.

Because God the Father loves His children, He does not want them to be tormented by fear, nor does He want them to fall into despair when calamity strikes. Accordingly, He bids us now to prepare for such times, so that we shall then receive all the help and comfort we need.

Who will experience this help and comfort? — He who has God on his side at such times. For when the almighty God, Creator of heaven and earth, is for us and contends for us, who or what could harm us? Then we have at our side the One to whom all power in heaven and on earth is given. And He will exercise this power on our behalf if we love Him. For Jesus has said that whoever loves Him will be loved by Him in return (John 14:21). And if God loves us, He will tenderly care for us, making it His concern to grant us protection and aid.

In the highly critical times to come everything depends upon whether we have a right to expect the Father's help, having received a child's rights by faith in Jesus Christ, to whom we have committed our lives.

Indeed, everything depends upon whether we love Him with all our hearts as true children. Then we may reckon with the fact that He will demonstrate His power and overwhelm His children with goodness, so that in times of affliction we shall be 'hidden' in Him and not be crushed by misery and distress, as one would normally expect. God's marvellous promises of help and protection in times of trouble will hold good for us.

However, the promise of protection does not necessarily imply deliverance from affliction or death. For some of His own a coming war, for instance, will bring great suffering or even the hour when the Lord calls them home. But it is equally true that in this time of distress, God's children will experience refuge, aid and divine care in a special way — indeed, miracles in the midst of suffering. Fear will give way and they will feel secure in the Father's arms. Their hearts imbued with peace and strength, they are able to endure everything. They experience how the Father in heaven cares for their smallest needs, how He thinks of them in hardship and danger and wards off evil. They experience that they are not at the mercy of human hands and weapons, but hidden in the Father's hands — despite all affliction. And if the Father has ordained their departure from life at this time, they will be borne upwards by the hands of angels or see the open heavens like Stephen.

The martyr Maximilian Kolbe is proof of this. Jesus lived in him to such an extent that an agonising death by starvation in the Auschwitz concentration camp (during World War II) did not drive him to despair and insanity as it did others. He was immersed in the peace of Jesus, his face radiant in the hour of his death. To the very end he sang unto his Lord.

In many cases, however, true children of God will literally experience wonderful instances of protection. This is especially promised to His chosen ones and has been their experience down through the ages. Indeed, 'the Lord knows how to rescue the godly from trial' (2 Pet. 2:9). They can expect this and firmly count on experiencing many divine miracles.

Do we belong to the 'godly'? Do we belong to those whose joy and delight is God alone and on whose behalf God will intervene? Is God for us? This is the most crucial question for us today. Woe betide us if He must stand against us because some unforgiven sin separates us from Him or because we are irreconciled with another person. If we dare to so enter the coming time of hardship, we shall look in vain for His help.

Destruction is threatening to descend; the time of His judgment has drawn near. The world is corrupt and, therefore, as was prophesied, God will be forced to execute judgment upon the earth. We all know that peril is imminent, since preparations for war steadily increase and the arms race is being stepped up. A nuclear war is threatening to break out — as well as a worldwide persecution of Christians. The persecution undergone by Christians in recent decades has assumed untold proportions, exceeding that of all previous centuries.

Jesus foretold that in the last times, 'You will be hated by all nations for my name's sake' (Matt. 24:9). We are inevitably entering upon the time when, as Christians, we shall be hated and persecuted everywhere. Are we prepared? Will God be on our side in the time of disaster, because we trust Him as true children of His, hating sin and confessing, 'Jesus Christ means everything to me'? Nothing can then separate us from Him, not even the most appalling events, for He is Life itself, and this life is peace and joy. When Christ is our life, the forces of death and hatred cannot crush us, for Jesus, who is stronger still, has already put them under His feet, and His peace will fill our hearts.

The impending time of severe affliction heralds the advent of this mighty Victor, this sovereign Ruler and Lord of lords. He is coming. In the depths of utter darkness and distress a glorious promise shines forth. 'The King is coming, the Bridegroom is approaching to gather His chosen ones to Himself and establish His kingdom.' Thus the time of affliction and distress actually ushers in His coming.

Yes, brighter than all the darkness is the radiant sun of promise, which, even in the midst of hardship, causes the bride of the Lamb — all those who truly love Him — to rejoice in the knowledge that the Bridegroom is coming! The challenge of the midnight hour is, 'Go out to meet the Bridegroom! He is coming!' Indeed, He comes even today to those who love Him. He comes to them in their distress. They gaze at Him and one single glance causes all the misery to fade into the background. They know that soon He will appear as King and end all their distress.

This assurance not only comforts those who love Jesus, but causes their souls to rise up on wings like eagles. They live in the glad hope and expectation of His coming and the celebration of the Marriage Feast of the Lamb.

Consequently, heaven comes down amid the darkness on earth and fills their hearts, letting them taste eternal joy. In them lives the jubilant cry that resounds while the blows of judgment are still descending, as John heard in the Revelation, 'The kingdom of the world has become the kingdom of our Lord and of his Christ, and he shall reign for ever and ever' (Rev. 11:15).

How to Deal with Fear

You may say to yourself: Fear devours me. Fear paralyses me. Fear — how can I master it?

It is like an incurable disease. Time and again it comes over me and keeps me from being happy.

Fear — what can I do about it?
Is there any way to get rid of it?

There is Someone who understands our fear. He is the One who bears and suffers it with us. For He says in the face of all impending calamities, 'In the world you have tribulation.' But He does not stop there — He goes on to say, 'Be of good cheer, I have overcome the world,' and since He has overcome the world, He has also overcome the fears in it.

What a prospect! What an opportunity! To Him is given all power and authority in heaven and on earth. When we call upon Him, He helps us. He also conquers our fear.

It is, therefore, vital that we bring Him our fear and proclaim ever anew His victorious name over it with the implicit faith that our fear must yield before this Lord. He is greater than all the fears and dangers that may assail us in this life. Just as long ago, the wind and waves are stilled by Him today. He is the One who can help us by comforting our fearful hearts and immersing them in peace when we call upon His name ever anew.

Yet our fear will not be taken from us in a single day merely because we once prayed to Jesus, 'Take away my fear.' It is essential that we keep on praying and battling in faith. And should we have to wait a long time, we have the assurance that Jesus will always prove Himself as Victor if we persist in prayer and faith. He will prove that He is mightier than our fear. Whoever concentrates on Jesus' victory at Calvary, instead of dwelling upon the lost battles in his fight against fear, will experience Jesus' victory in this area too.

Release from fear! Let us make this the firm objective of our faith in view of the time of affliction that lies ahead of us, and say:

I believe that You will conquer my fear, Jesus, before the time of disaster comes. I firmly cling to this aim of faith. Every day I will bring it before You in prayer.

How could He not answer such a prayer? Jesus has come to save us, so that we 'might serve him without fear' (Luke 1:74). If Jesus sets us free, we are free indeed — free from fear and immersed in His peace in the midst of distress. Jesus has the power to transform our hearts, so that they are filled with comfort and peace instead of fear, and resting in God's love and care.

Indeed, we may know for sure that the Father is taking care of us. His eyes are resting upon us. His love and care are ours. He will cradle us in His arms and keep us 'in his shelter in the day of trouble'. He will command His mighty hosts of angels to surround us.

Let us trust Him. We shall experience miracles of protection and acts of goodness if we battle in faith against our fear, calling upon the victorious name of Jesus and trusting in the Father's love. This we shall experience as truly as God keeps His promises.

He delivers the needy when he
calls, the poor and him who has no
helper.

Psalm 72:12

And it shall come to pass
that all who call upon the name
of the Lord shall be delivered.

Joel 2:32

In Jesus Christ's almighty name
All fears are put to flight.
Their pow'r is broken by the
   mighty Victor, Jesus.

I praise aloud in faith today
That fear can reign no more.
The pow'r of fear lies vanquished
   at the feet of Jesus.

Fear can no longer rule my heart,
For Christ is stronger still.
At Jesus' word all fears are quelled
   and made to vanish.

From my heart every fear departs
And peace comes in to stay,
The perfect peace that Jesus won for me
   at Calv'ry.

I praise aloud that I am free,
Harassed by fear no more;
For in His peace Christ Jesus lets me
   rest securely.

I claim in faith that Jesus Christ
Will set me free from fear.
This miracle He will perform
   to His great glory.

Comfort and Advice for Times of Fear

Are you afraid? Then be assured: God the Father is especially concerned about His fearful children. To them in particular He sends angels to strengthen, comfort, calm and help them.

Fearful children can take the Father at His word:

> You are all round me on every side;
> you protect me with your power.
>
> Psalm 139:5 GNB

An earthly father carries his fearful child in his arms. God the Father will do the same and even more for you. Therefore, in view of the coming hardships you can rejoice and say:

> He will hide me in his shelter in the day
>   of trouble;
> he will conceal me under the cover
>   of his tent.
>
> Psalm 27:5

Is your fear great? Then pronounce this word ever anew, 'Father, my Father!'

Say to Him, 'I trust You. You will carry me through.' And consolation, peace and security will flow into your heart.

If your fear is great, there is Someone greater still who can conquer it —

Jesus Christ!

Call upon Him!

All my fear to You I'm bringing,
Ever of Your vict'ry singing,
For You conquered every fear.
I will trust You, dearest Jesus,
Firmly standing on Your promise
That You've overcome the world.

Yes, the world with all its terrors
Has to yield to You, my Saviour.
You have vanquished it indeed.
Thus no horrors can o'ertake me.
Every terror must forsake me,
For, O Lord, You are my shield.

May You ever stand before me
As the mighty Prince of Vict'ry,
Lord o'er hardships, tumults, wars.
With Your shield You will protect me,
Then I'll see Your image only;
Fear and horror will depart.

The Way to Overcome

Are you afraid? Then ask yourself why.

Usually the real reason is a lack of dedication to the will of God and unwillingness to suffer — an attitude that is closely related to a lack of trust in the love of God.

Are you afraid of losing your possessions?

Then surrender everything to God beforehand, and your soul will find peace. Moreover, trust that He will care for you, and you will be comforted.

Are you afraid of losing loved ones?

Commit yourself to God in the willingness to suffer the loss of dear ones. Surrender yourself in the confidence that Jesus, who loves you more than words can tell, will then draw near to you and grant you His love as never before — and you will be comforted.

Are you afraid of hunger, want and poverty?

Then say, 'I am willing to bear all this, my Father. I commit myself to hardship in the assurance that I can do all things in Jesus

Christ, who strengthens me. I shall know how to face plenty, or hunger and want, for He will give me the strength to endure.'

Are you afraid of physical suffering?

Then say, 'I will endure suffering, looking unto You, Lord Jesus, the suffering Lamb of God. One glance at You in faith, O Man of Sorrows, strengthens me to bear my suffering in love for You.'

Are you afraid of seeing loved ones suffer?

Then say, 'Because I know You love them more than I do, I believe You will come to their aid.' And thank the Father for the assurance that their suffering will bring them great glory for all eternity.

Are you afraid that your old sinful self will get the better of you in the time of hardship and distress?

Then fight now the battle of faith against all your sinful traits, and God will reward you in the time of disaster. He will grant you special strength in accordance with the demands placed on you, so that you will be able to overcome.

*He will cover you
with his pinions,
and under his wings
you will find refuge.*

Psalm 91:4

Don't Try to Repress Fear,
But Talk to God about It

My dear Father,

I thank You that I may come to You with my fear, for You are the best father there is. Therefore, You understand Your child and are compassionate towards him when he is afraid.

My Father, I thank You for the knowledge that as my Father You will help me. You will strengthen my soul and take away my fear.

I thank You that I belong to You as Your child. No calamity can separate me from You. Your hand will guide me through all hardships.

I thank You and rejoice, for You, my Father, always have help ready for Your child. I cling to this promise in all my fears and distress. You will not disappoint me.

I thank You and rejoice, for in all my fears I shall experience Jesus as the Victor, who will command fear to depart and say to me, 'My peace be with you.'

I thank You that when uprisings, rumours of war and the prospect of a terrible nuclear war seek to frighten me, You will be like a wall of fire round about me, just as You say in Your Word. Then fear will not be able to take hold of me.

I thank You that I may firmly reckon with one fact: In the time of great affliction, even if I lose everything, I shall never lose You, my Father. And since You are the sovereign Lord, who possesses all power in heaven and on earth, who has everything in His hands and who is able to accomplish everything, I have everything that I need in You. Abba, dearest Father!   Amen.

Release!

Shortly before the outbreak of war in 1939, I assumed a travelling ministry, which led me to many different parts of Germany where I held missionary lectures and Bible study courses. This meant undertaking perilous journeys throughout the war, for the trains — at least during the latter part of the war — were often threatened by low-flying aircraft. Above all, air raids were made on many of the cities where I was scheduled to hold lectures in the evenings. Though very apprehensive by nature, I was, amazingly enough, able to undertake these dangerous journeys in peace. My fear was overcome and I was able to perform with gladness this ministry, which, humanly speaking, was so very difficult for me.

What was the key to this inner comfort and peace of mind? Six or seven years prior to this ministry, I had a travelling ministry for the Women's Division of the German Student Christian Movement. Since I suffered greatly from rheumatism and often endured much pain at night, especially in unfavourable lodgings, this work was not to my liking. I sometimes sighed to myself and dreaded ever having to resume such a ministry. Later I came to a deep repentance over this fear, which stemmed from reluctance to bear the cross. I was ashamed of my fear, for it became clear to me that service for Jesus should be done with joy, and if we can add sacrifices to it, we should be grateful, for such sacrifices make our service a blessing and fruitful.

Sensing this lack of dedication on my part, I asked the Lord to give me another chance to prove my love and willingness to sacrifice. The Lord gave me an opportunity by entrusting me with another travelling ministry — this time during the difficult war years. I then experienced the power that lies in contrition: it changes our hearts and evokes new spiritual life and love for Jesus. This love, in turn, banishes fear and makes difficult tasks easy. Contrition and love for Jesus now made me regard it a privilege to have a travelling ministry again. Now I had learnt to say the words of love to Jesus, 'For You! For You!' whenever I encountered difficulties and perils while travelling. These words brought peace into my heart and made the bitter sweet, for love transforms everything. This love, born of contrition and repentance, enabled me to trust the Lord and say, 'You have set me free from fear. You will carry me through. You will not let me be tested beyond my strength.'

And so it happened. He carried me through and gave me His peace. He proved Himself as Victor over fear. Yes, He let me experience wonderful instances of protection.

Indeed, in many cases repentance is the way to release from fear, which often stems from reluctance to bear the cross and unwillingness to make sacrifices. Contrition and repentance drive us to Jesus and cause us to claim His act of salvation and to praise the power of His redemptive blood. This in turn brings us release — yes, release from fear — and renewal for our lives. Then that which we previously feared is no longer a source of dread. Strengthened and comforted, we are able to endure the very thing that we used to be afraid of. This I have experienced as a reality.

I prayed to the Lord,
and he answered me;
he freed me from all my fears.

Psalm 34:4 GNB

I will trust You, dearest Father;
You're my Helper and Adviser;
You can transform all my needs.
I will trust, though storms are raging
And my cares around me surging,
Leaving no way out for me.

O my Father, You will guide me;
You've prepared the help already.
You will ne'er forsake Your child.
You look after me in goodness
And You plan in loving-kindness
How to help me in my need.

I will trust You, O my Father,
For Your help will fail me never.
I can count upon Your aid.
So I thank You, dearest Father,
For Your promise stands for ever
And Your name is Yea — Amen.

Training for Tomorrow

In Times of Distress and Calamity

— you will experience the Father in heaven in the same measure that you have borne His image in your heart.

— you will be able to go through the dark vale of fears and perils if you have learnt the secret of trusting and applied it in the minor difficulties and problems of today.

— you will be able to overcome in fear and suffering and even be a source of comfort and encouragement to others to the extent that you have asked Jesus for the patient, enduring love of the Lamb beforehand and allowed Him to transform you into His image.

— you will experience God's overwhelming love and care and divine aid if you love Him now and keep His commandments.

Not Fatherless

Do we know what it means for a child to be fatherless — to have no one who will lovingly comfort him?

To be fatherless is to be without protection.

To be fatherless is to have no father who will safely carry his child through everything on his strong arms.

To be fatherless is to have no father who will attend to his child's every need and provide for him.

To be fatherless is to have no father who will show concern when his child is hurt and seek to ease his pain.

To be fatherless is to have no father who hears every cry of his child and hastens to soothe and comfort his child and dry his tears.

Yes, whoever is fatherless is at the mercy of all

evil powers and dangers, exposed to hunger
and all manner of needs.

> But we are not fatherless!
> God is our Father!

> And He loves us more than all earthly
> fathers taken together — He is indeed
> the 'Father of the fatherless' (Ps. 68:5).

Never alone in pain and fear
Are they who trust the Father dear
And call on Him.

In love He watches over you,
Planning what He will give and do
For you, His child.

Be of good cheer, He knows a way;
The Lord, your Saviour, on you lays
His loving hand.

Though He seems far from you, His child,
He's one with you in love so mild.
O trust, He's here!

The Father Himself loves you.

John 16:27

Can a woman forget her sucking child, that she should have no compassion on the son of her womb?
Even these may forget,
yet I will not forget you.

Isaiah 49:15

Fear Not, God Is Your Father

If by faith in Jesus Christ, our Saviour, we have become children of God and have His Spirit within us, we may lay claim to the rights of God's children. When in need we can cry, 'Father! Father!' And the Father will fulfil His responsibility as a father. His fatherly love moves Him to answer our cries. He is constrained to come to us when we are in distress. He is compelled to aid us and help us out of our troubles, for He is indeed our Father, a true Father!

It is not merely a sense of duty but fatherly love that constrains our Father to take us into His arms in tender love like small children and press us close to Him until all our fear has vanished.

Let us think highly of the Father's love and might. Then He will prove them to us. He will not remain far away, but come when His child is in distress. At such times He will be closer to His child than ever. The Father Himself will ward off all lurking dangers that threaten to harm His child or lead him into peril. He will intervene on behalf of His child. For a child is weak, a child is helpless, a child has neither power nor authority — *but the Father does!* He exerts His power on behalf of His child when he is in need. For He dearly loves His child. What a wonderful Father we have in God!

When Wilt Thou Comfort Me?

'When wilt thou comfort me?' Thus asked the psalmist in the midst of affliction. We might ask the same question in this age of death. We are anxious to receive comfort and ask whether it will be granted us. But there is no shadow of doubt about it being granted — God has prepared us a cup of comfort, filled to the brim, for Holy Scripture calls Him 'the God of all comfort'. And because God is a Father, there is no concern dearer to His heart than to comfort His children in times of affliction and situations of distress. The Apostle Paul, whose life was filled with suffering, could testify to the 'God of all comfort, who comforts us in all our affliction' (2 Cor. 1:3f.).

There is only one hindrance that can prevent the Father from pouring His cup of comfort into our hearts. And that is if our hearts are closed. Closed, because they are filled with mistrust and rebellion against the suffering God has laid upon us. Closed, because we are irreconciled, unmerciful and critical towards our brother. Closed, because of unforgiven sins that are known to us. Such a heart is incapable of receiving comfort.

Let us hear the Father's plea today in view of the impending calamities, 'Bring Me your rebelliousness, your unforgiving spirit. Bring Me every sin. I will cast them behind My back' (cf. Isa. 38:17). In answering this call, you will experience that the Lord has compassion on you. Comfort will fill your heart like balsam being poured into a wound. You no longer need fear the coming time of affliction, for when you are comforted, suffering loses its sting and it is no longer hard to bear. Peace and everlasting joy will then fill your heart amid the greatest suffering. You will be consoled.

My help comes from the Lord,
who made heaven and earth.
Psalm 121:2

My Father, I Will . . .

My Father,

I will always trust You, because You are so good.

My Father,

I will always give thanks to You, even for hardships, because in Your heart You have lovingly planned that they bring me a special blessing.

My Father,

Committing myself to You, I will submit to all the chastenings necessary to prepare me for the time of great distress. Create in me patience, trust, a sacrificial spirit and willingness to suffer, so that I shall be able to endure the hardships in the time of affliction.

My Father,

I will always believe that You are greater than every hardship, that You can do everything and that You love me.

My Father,

I will always look to You — and You alone.

Amen.

O Father, dearest Father,
Within Your hands I rest.
Lord, You can transform all things;
All power You possess.

I rest in You, safe hidden,
O dearest Father mine.
When fears and cares surround me,
In You deep peace I find.

Within Your heart I'm resting;
Your love enfolds me there.
Your heart knows all my suff'ring
And how much I can bear.

All that will come upon me
I know You've planned, O Lord.
The suff'ring that You send me
Serves only to my good.

My heart in fear and sorrow
May rest in quietness.
I trust in Your will wholly
And this is blessèdness.

Reckon with the Father

Whoever reckons solely with human resources in times of affliction will be overwhelmed by fear and distress. He will not experience any help. But whoever counts on the miracles of God will experience help and comfort — victory over his fears.

Declare aloud in word and song who the heavenly Father is:

> Love that cares,
> that watches over His child.

> Almighty Love, whose powerful arm
> is outstretched over His child.

> Compassionate Love
> that carries His fearful child
> through all hardships and perils.

> All-transforming Love
> that changes darkness into light
> and hell into heaven.

Never-ending Love
that surrounds His children
at all times and in all places.

By praising God's fatherly love, you will experience help in your fears.

You have always been my help.
In the shadow of your wings
I sing for joy.
                    Psalm 63:7 GNB

I Fear No Evil, For Thou Art with Me

spiritual weapons to combat
all fears of peril, revolution,
persecution and nuclear war

In Holy Scripture God gives us verses, special promises, which in time of peril and hardship we can use like weapons to combat the enemy, so that comfort, peace and courage will enter into our hearts. The Book of Psalms, in particular, is a real treasure chest of such verses. Why is that so? The reason is that these verses have been tried and tested in life — they were born out of extreme fear, persecution and peril.

Let us consider King David who, prior to the time he ascended the throne, lived in constant peril, in the midst of wars and uprisings, endangered by his enemies, persecutors and opponents. He had discovered that these words brought him help and victory when he spoke them aloud or sang them. These were verses in which he described the nature of God, declaring what He can do and what He desires. Tremendous power lies in them, as King David experienced. For, ever anew we read in the Psalms that he would burst forth in a canticle of praise. How tremendous it is to be able to break through to praise in moments of fear and distress! Thus these words that David declared aloud or sang in the sight of heaven and hell have been tried and proved. They have power. They are preserved for us in the Bible and are there for us, so that we too may use them in times of distress and experience their power.

Let us join King David in saying, for instance, 'Thou, O Lord, art a shield for me' (Ps. 3:3 AV). In those days a warrior was protected if he held up a shield before himself; then the enemy's weapons could not strike him. He was covered. Therefore, say aloud, 'Thou, O Lord, art a shield for me!' — and believe it. Repeat it two or three times, stressing the word 'art'. 'Thou, O Lord, *art* a shield for me!' That is to say, 'It's true. In times of old and again today You are a shield. You protect me. When You place Yourself before me, the destructive forces, revolutionaries, persecutors or nuclear weapons cannot penetrate this defence.'

Now shift the emphasis, saying, 'Thou, O Lord, art a *shield*!' In other words, You are the One who provides me with complete coverage from all the calamities that could befall me. Not only do all suffering and affliction first have to pass by You, the almighty God, but when You Yourself are covering me, they cannot strike me. For then I am hidden in You.

Repeat the words of this verse in song and praise. 'Thou, O Lord, art a shield for *me*! — yes, for me personally, in the particular fears and perils I have to suffer. This I shall experience and thereby join the ranks of those who have testified to the reality of this truth since David's time.'

We can also praise God for truly being a Helper, as it says in another psalm:

> God is our refuge and strength, a very present help in trouble.
>
> Psalm 46:1

These too are majestic words. They stand like solid rock. Say the verse for yourself, 'God is *my* refuge and strength, a very present help for *me* when *I* am in the midst of trouble.' Hold it up against all the powers threatening you from within and without, and you will discover that help will come, as it is written:

> My help comes from the Lord, who made heaven and earth.
>
> Psalm 121:2

Take such a verse as a promissory note that the Lord has given you and that He will make good. Take it as a definite promise and hold it out to the Lord, saying, 'It is written that "Thou art my help" (Ps. 40:17). And therefore I firmly reckon with Your help, for Your name is Yea and Amen. You cannot deny Yourself. You are a Father and cannot but help and deliver Your child.'

Only if you reckon with God in this manner and only if you picture Him in your heart in His fatherly love as a Helper and Deliverer, will you experience His help. For our experience with God corresponds to the concept we bear of Him in our hearts, just as King David says in one of his psalms:

> With the kind and merciful You will show Yourself kind and merciful; with an upright man You will show Yourself upright ... and with the perverse You will show Yourself contrary.
>
> Psalm 18:25 f. AB

In other words, the 'perverse' did not believe that God would do anything good for them or bring them help. With such an attitude they erected a barrier between themselves and the love of God, which He would have poured out upon them. As a result they cannot really experience His love and for the same reason they receive no help. Do we ever consider the fact that it depends on us whether or not we experience God's help? It lies ready in store for us, but it can be granted only to those whose hearts are open and inclined towards God and who do not raise a barrier against Him by their mistrust.

Therefore, express your trust in God's omnipotence and goodness by repeating the words:

> The Lord is my rock, and my fortress, and my deliverer, my God, my rock, in whom I take refuge, my shield, and the horn of my salvation, my stronghold.
>
> Psalm 18:2

There is great power in declaring aloud what God means to you. He is your protection, a fortress in which you can take refuge, and this reality holds true for you. According to the reports of some believers, there were instances in war time when enemy soldiers pushed their way into a room where people were praying, stood transfixed and then left, frightened away by the power of the presence of God. They were unable to carry out their wicked plans. The believers were in God's fortress, surrounded by hosts of angels who fought on their behalf.

Or repeat aloud the name that David gives to the Lord time and again in the psalms:

My deliverer. Psalm 18:2

Say, 'Because You are my Deliverer, I shall wait expectantly for deliverance when I am in distress.' Say again and again:

My God, my strength,
in whom I will trust.

Psalm 18:2 AV

Yes, say to the Lord with the utmost conviction, 'I trust in You!' Then you will experience that

None who have faith in God will ever be disgraced for trusting him.

Psalm 25:3 LB

Write down all such verses from the Psalms as precious offers of His love. We should begin to use them now, speaking or singing them repeatedly whenever fear strikes us and thus have them on hand for the time of great affliction, calamity and trial that will come upon the whole world. Then we shall be victorious. And when that time comes, we shall experience that His Word has power to dispel all fears and even put enemies to flight. The peace of God will descend upon us, and we shall be granted help and deliverance.

Why are you cast down, O my soul, and why are you disquieted within me? Hope in God; for I shall again praise him, my help and my God.

Psalm 43:5

God Takes Care of His Own

Our dear Father,

We thank You that we may call upon You on behalf of our loved ones. We are concerned about them, since they are approaching great danger and hardship or already undergoing it. You are a Father of mercy and the God of all comfort. And therefore we trust in You and believe that You will surround them with Your protection and loving care and that You will cause rivers of divine comfort to flow into their hearts. Fill their hearts with divine peace and enable them to be a source of comfort and a tower of strength in their surroundings, and for many a fearful heart a living testimony as to who You are — the Father of all comfort.

We thank You that when we think of our loved ones we can rest assured, since You will make the words come true, 'The greater the hardship, the nearer God is.' We thank You for the knowledge that nothing can happen to them except that which You have ordained and which serves to their good. And You will not let them be tempted beyond their strength.

Once again, we give thanks that You are our

Father, who hears the cries of the afflicted and comes to the aid of the oppressed. Therefore, we bring You all our anxiety about our dear ones who are in distress. If You are with them, they have all that they need — Your love and care are sufficient. Amen.

In days of suff'ring,
Of fear and trembling,
My heart will praise God's faithfulness.

In God I'm trusting,
On His word standing.
He will fulfil it in His time.

For this I'll thank You
And ever trust You,
In sorrow never wavering.

You are my Father,
My loving Counsellor,
In every sorrow helping me.

My will and yearnings
I'll still by trusting
In Your will, which is always good.

*The Lord knows how to rescue
the godly from trial.*

2 Peter 2:9

*With the Lord on my side I do not
fear. The Lord is on my side
to help me.*

Psalm 118:6 f.

Ours For Ever

What is it that cannot be lost when we lose all else in the coming times? — The Lord God! If you have Him, you have everything that you need, even in the midst of fear and distress.

Therefore, in times of peril make sure that God is for you.

If God is against you because of uncleansed sin in your life, you will be lost when disaster strikes.

If God is for you because you submit to His holiness ever anew, nothing can harm you! You will experience comfort and help.

If God is for us, who is against us?
For I am sure that neither death,
nor life, nor angels, nor princi-
palities, nor things present, nor
things to come, nor powers, nor
height, nor depth, nor anything else
in all creation, will be able to sepa-
rate us from the love of God in
Christ Jesus our Lord.

Romans 8:31, 38 f.

The All-important Question for the Time of Affliction: 'Can God Be for Me or Does He Have to Be against Me?'

Let us ask ourselves:

Can God be for me
— because I respect His will, His commandments, taking them as the standard for my life?
— because I ask forgiveness every time I break His commandments, every time I sin against God and man, and claim the blood of Jesus in the battle of faith, so that I might be cleansed of my sinful traits?

If there is no unforgiven sin known to me that could separate me from God, He will let me rest in His arms in the time of affliction, and I shall experience His loving care, protection and help.

Does God have to be against me
— because I am too proud to ask what His will is when I make decisions?
— because I don't obey His commandments?
— because I deliberately persist in sin?
— because I do not confess my guilt?

— because I do not fight against my sins in the name of Jesus and in the power of His blood?

If so, my unforgiven sins will separate me from God in the time of affliction. Instead of experiencing His fatherly love and help I shall then experience His judgment and wrath.

Can God be for me
— because I am for my brother, that is, because I show merciful, forgiving love towards everyone, including those who do me wrong?

— because I live in peace and reconciliation with them in gratitude that I, who have sinned against God, have been reconciled with Him by the sacrifice of Jesus?

If so, God will intervene on my behalf in the time of affliction, granting me His power and aid, and I shall experience His miracles.

Does God have to be against me
— because I close my heart to my brother and erect a barrier against those whom I find hard to bear or who have wronged me?

If so, God will have to erect a barrier against me and will no longer be able to grant me forgiveness. Thus He will not be able to act on my behalf in the time of great affliction.

Can God be for me

— because I make my will one with His and humble myself beneath His mighty hand, even in difficult leadings?

— because I trust that God knows what is best for His child and acknowledge that as a sinful being I need to be chastened by the hand of the Father?

Then I shall experience in the time of affliction that God gives grace to the humble and I shall find help.

Does God have to be against me

— because in my pride and defiance I rebel against His leadings when I am in suffering instead of humbling myself beneath His will?

Then I shall find that God opposes the proud. In the time of affliction I shall experience neither comfort, nor help, nor peace.

Promises for Those Who Love Him

Because he cleaves to me in love, I will deliver him; I will protect him, because he knows my name. When he calls to me, I will answer him; I will be with him in trouble, I will rescue him and honour him.

Psalm 91:14 f.

They shall feed along the ways, on all bare heights shall be their pasture; they shall not hunger or thirst, neither scorching wind nor sun shall smite them, for he who has pity on them will lead them, and by springs of water will guide them.

Isaiah 49:9 ff.

In Times of Peril and Destruction What Awaits Those Who Love God?

Comfort from the Father,
who takes His fearful, trembling child into His
arms and embraces him with great love.

Loving words from the Father,
which are like balsam flowing into the fearful
soul.

Union with the Father and the Lord Jesus
as never before. For nothing can separate us
from God — neither affliction, nor fear, nor
hardship. On the contrary, all these will serve
only to bind us closer to Him.

A strong guard of angels
protecting God's own on all sides and minister-
ing unto them.

Miracles of God too numerous to be counted,
miracles that God performs for His chosen ones
— today as long ago — in times of great affliction, as we can see from the history of His
people Israel.

The experience that Jesus is greater
than every hardship, every torment, and the
victorious assurance that we are in His hands
alone and not in the hands of men.

Peace like a river,
which God causes to flow into our hearts, so
that all fear must yield.

The open heavens,
for heaven will come down like never before to
God's own and open up to them when night on
earth is at its darkest.

A special endowment of power and strength
in these hard times for God's own to pass
through all the hardship and suffering as over-
comers.

The presence of Jesus,
more real than ever before. He will illumine the
night with the brightness of His love and turn
hell into heaven.

For in His Word we have the promise:

> Those who love me I love,
> those who search for me find me.
> I endow with riches those who love me
> and I will fill their treasuries.
>
> Proverbs 8:17,21 NEB

The Triumphant Assurance of Faith

Lord,
I thank You for the comforting assurance that nothing can harm me when Your almighty hand covers me.

Lord,
I thank You for the certainty that in times of extreme need You will reveal Yourself to me as the One to whom the 'wind and waves' of destruction are subject.

Lord,
I praise You now in advance, for I know that the greater the calamity and destruction are, the greater Your help and love will prove to be.

Lord,
One thing I firmly believe: when great fear clutches at my heart on the day of terror and threatens to consume me, Your peace and comfort will be greater still.

Lord,
I trust in Your love, which will care for me in

the midst of all the frightening events. Like a father You will take me by the hand when the path leads into darkness.

Lord,
How wonderful that I may trust in Your love, whose power and ability to help are far greater than the forces of destruction!

Lord,
Let me firmly expect that as a loving Father You will prepare for me, Your child, a table in the presence of my enemies, in the midst of hardships.

Lord,
In the face of the impending destruction let me look only unto You, for You are on Your way to establish Your kingdom.

Lord,
I will trust in Your power to work miracles and You will let me experience them in the time of affliction and destruction.

Lord,
I refuse to dwell upon the coming horrors; rather I will think of You and Your love.

Lord,

I believe that the Holy Spirit will guide me when there is no one else to show me the next step.

Lord,

Let me trust You and firmly expect that in the time of great affliction You will turn hell into heaven because Your presence will transform everything. Amen.

The angel of the Lord encamps around those who fear him, and delivers them.

Psalm 34:7

A Strong Guard of Angels

God can never do enough when it comes to helping His beloved children and attending to their needs — especially in times of hardship and calamity. He sends out His mighty messengers to carry out His commands. Like a strong wall the angels surround His children — that is, those who fear Him and call upon Him, their Father, in every distress.

We are never alone. At all times the angels are about us and engaged in warfare against Satan and all the evil spirits who are raging across the earth now in the last times in order to cause havoc. The angelic hosts are a reality. The holy angels watch over us. They live to serve us. The more the time of affliction and destruction closes in on us, the more active they are in using their heavenly power and might. They work zealously to overcome difficulties, ward off severe perils, and intervene so that we might experience protection.

Let us pray ever anew to our heavenly Father for protection by this guard of angels. Let us count on it and thank Him for commanding His angels to protect us. Then we shall experience protection.

He will give his angels charge of
you to guard you in all your ways.
Psalm 91:11

What are the angels, then?
They are spirits who serve God
and are sent by him to help those
who are to receive salvation.
Hebrews 1:14 GNB

Trust Brings Joy to the Heart of God

Entrust yourself to God
just as a child would entrust himself
to his father,
and you will experience
that even in the darkest of moments
He will not fail you.

In *every* fear and hardship
turn to God with childlike trust
and you will make the Father's heart rejoice,
for He is waiting to hear you call,
'Abba, dearest Father!'

Behold, we call those happy who were steadfast.
You have heard of the steadfastness of Job, and
you have seen the purpose of the Lord, how the
Lord is compassionate and merciful.

James 5:11

What Will Help You When All Is Dark?

The knowledge that the Father is greater than everything.

The joy of being dependent upon the Father.

Implicit, childlike trust.

Total dedication to the Father.

Desiring nothing else but the Father —
and Him alone.

Being content with that
which the Father provides.

Immersing your will in the Father's will.

Saying when you cannot understand His ways,
'I trust You!'

What else can help you?

The faith that the Father always has a way to help you.

The knowledge that the Father loves you with an ineffable love.

The joyful assurance of being hidden in the Father's hands at all times.

The promise that you are being led according to an eternal plan, which will bring you to the heavenly goal.

Dearest Lord, I trust Your leadings,
Though the way seems dark to me.
On such paths I'll find great blessing
Hidden in the suffering.

Dearest Lord, I know You love me,
Though I do not understand.
Lord, I trust that You are guiding,
Though I cannot see Your hand.

I believe Your hand is guiding,
And at work in everything.
You are Love, and thus You only
Can have thoughts of good for me.

*Yea, though I walk
through the valley
    of the shadow
    of death,
I will fear no evil:
    for thou art with me.*

Psalm 23:4 AV

Held by His Hands

Our Lord Jesus Christ says,

> No one shall snatch them out of my hand.
> John 10:28

> My hands of love are holding you,
> The hands that did so much for you,
> Were pierced upon the cross.
> I am beside you every hour,
> And shall reveal My love and pow'r
> When you are in distress.

In love we respond:

> Lord, here I am. You bore the cross
> And You will not abandon us.
> You'll help me bear it bravely.
> You see how weak and small I am,
> But with You I can overcome.
> I trust that You will help me.

A Prayer for the Time of Christian Persecution and Martyrdom

O Jesus,

May You be my sole possession today in joy and suffering, so that in the hour of affliction You will be for me the source of all comfort and love, constraining me to follow You wherever You go.

Grant that I shall never part from You, nor choose relief at the cost of losing You, but always choose You, even in the midst of torment and affliction.

May the hour of trial find this love burning in my heart, so that I may comfort You, glorify Your name and make it known to many others.

In Your love You will not forsake me — this I know. And when the critical moment comes, I shall receive what I have prayed for. Your faithfulness is my protection and shield.   Amen.

Mother Martyria

What power lies in love for Jesus! It alone is indestructible in times of affliction, for it is aflame with divine fire. When this ardour burns in a heart, its flames are stronger than the flames of hell, which seek to destroy body, soul and spirit. Yes, this love even has the power to extinguish pain and torment.

For Your Sake

Our dear Lord Jesus,

We thank You that Your special love belongs to those who are not only suffering in the ordinary sense, but who are suffering for Your name's sake out of love for You. We thank You that we may trust in Your love to carry us through such suffering.

We thank You, Lord Jesus, for the knowledge that at the close of the age You want to walk across this earth once again — this time in Your own. You long for them to reflect You in Your patience, Your forgiving love towards Your enemies, and Your willingness to suffer when they, like You, are persecuted, tormented and ostracised. You will enable them to reflect You, for You manifest Your glory here on earth in the midst of suffering. You will demonstrate that You live in Your own. And because You live in them, Your image — the image of the Lamb, the image of suffering Love that blesses others — will be seen in them. Grant that by their example they may overcome some of Your enemies. Yes, grant that this love may be shed abroad and may help to pave the way for Your kingdom to come. We praise You, because the power of Your love is stronger than the powers of darkness that seem to rule the earth. In the end Your love will triumph.

We pray, pour Your powerful love into our hearts now as we follow the path of the Lamb in everyday life, so that in the time of affliction we shall overcome in all the suffering and persecution, because You are living in us. Help us to prepare now as we undergo the minor troubles and sorrows of today, so that we shall be equipped for the time of great affliction. Grant that we shall then glorify You by our lives and be a comfort and joy to You. Let us suffer in love for You, giving thanks for the honour to endure hatred and persecution for Your name's sake.

Teach us to suffer in true humility, ever conscious that we deserve far greater suffering because of our sins — and help us to show perfect love towards our enemies in the midst of suffering. May Your love, Lord Jesus, triumph in us.

Amen.

With You the cross' way I'll go,
With You I'll share its pain and woe,
With You go into darkness.
With You one day I shall arise,
Be throned with You in Paradise,
With You I am united.

With You I'll suffer pain and death,
With You I'll draw my final breath,
In life and death — with You, Lord!
And then with You — all sorrow past —
I'll soar to heights of joy at last
To dwell with You for ever.

With You, O dearest Lord, with You —
What harm can hell and suff'ring do?
You calm the stormy raging.
Though deepest suff'ring I may face,
Your heart shall be my resting place.
I'm one with You, my Jesus.

The Plans God Makes Are Wise

(Isa. 28:29 GNB)

My Father,

Help me to accept with a humble and trusting heart the sufferings and hardships that You send me now and those the future may hold for me. Help me to bear them in the knowledge that a difficult situation has never been mastered by despairing, but always by trusting.

Let me also trust You when Your leadings for my loved ones, for my nation and other nations, indeed, for the whole world, become harder and harder. Let me keep my eyes fixed on the final outcome, for Your pathways always end in glory. I thank You for the assurance that all Your leadings have been conceived according to an eternal and wonderful plan. They are directed towards a glorious goal and even if the way first leads through the night — through personal brokenness and judgment upon the nations — the outcome will be a new world, which You will create out of the ruins.

Therefore, with my eyes fixed on the goal, I will live in implicit trust and in the assurance

that after the chaos and affliction, Your glory
will dawn — and with it a new world.   Amen.

*I consider that the sufferings
of this present time are not worth
comparing with the glory that is to
be revealed to us.*

Romans 8:18

The Only Important Thing

Let me see the goal before me,
Dwelling not upon my suff'ring,
Heeding neither cross nor grief.
To Your throne I'll haste unswerving,
Pay no heed to cross and suff'ring,
Ever look to heaven's goal.

Let me see the goal before me,
Take my cross and follow daily,
Going with You to the end.
Let me say, 'Yes, Father' always,
Giving thanks that blessing follows,
Heeding not the cross' weight.

Let me see the goal before me
And extol the future glory
That You will bestow one day.
At Your throne I'll stand in glory
When my cross, Lord, has transformed me
And has brought me to the goal.

Let me see the goal before me.
Life on earth is over quickly;
Soon eternity will dawn.
There, by suffering ennobled,
In Your grace I'll be rewarded
With an everlasting crown.

Look to the Goal

My Father,

Help me always to live with my eternal home in mind. Open my eyes to see the goal, the glory that awaits me for all eternity. Let my primary concern be to reach this goal.

Teach me to put all earthly suffering in its proper perspective, even the severest suffering that could come upon me in the time of affliction. It is transient and, like the other things of this world, it will come to an end and pass away. But then eternity will follow. You have prepared an eternal home for me, and after all the suffering I shall find heavenly joy awaiting me in Your kingdom — joy that will last for ever and ever. Let me look ahead to this. Let my soul be absorbed by this thought. I will give my utmost to attain this goal, and so I shall willingly undergo the purifying process of suffering, which will prepare me for heaven. I want to live with my thoughts centred on eternity and not on the time of disaster, which is brief and will come to an end. I trust in Your goodness. You have measured exactly all the hardships of this age and know how much I am able to bear.

I thank You that in giving me this outlook, You are making me strong, so that I can bravely endure the dark stretches of the pathway and say in every hardship, 'I do not account my life of any value nor as precious to myself, if only I may accomplish my course' (Acts 20:24). Amen.

Now
   when these things
begin to take place,
look up
and raise your heads,
because your
   redemption
is drawing near.

Luke 21:28

Rejoice!
After Suffering Comes Heavenly Glory

Lift up your heads in the midst of affliction and darkness, for the great sufferings of our times proclaim that the hour of redemption is drawing near.

The darkest pathways of God will end in inconceivable joy for you when you pass through the heavenly gates. And for the whole world they will one day culminate in the appearance of His glory.

You may look forward to a day of supreme joy. Therefore, live now in the future glory — and you will taste heaven even in the midst of affliction.

The appalling circumstances on earth are not permanent. The final outcome will be peace, joy and divine glory in the Kingdom of God. Think on these things. Set your heart and mind on them.

Do not live in the present, in all your fears and cares, but rather live in the future — namely, in the heavenly glory, for which you are now being prepared.

Look not at the darkness in and about you; rather look at the rising Sun, which is Jesus, the Sun of suns. He seeks to draw you into His kingdom of light.

Let Jesus, the centre of heaven, be the centre of your life — the magnet that draws you. Then you will experience in the midst of suffering that no one can rob you of heaven, of Jesus Himself.

Rejoice! You are going out to meet Him. He is coming.

Who can measure the great treasure
Suffering and grief have brought?
Who has sight and understanding
For the good that suff'ring wrought?

Only those who sowed in sorrow
And came out of deepest night
Will be crowned as kings in glory,
Shining forth in splendour bright.

Who may live there close to Jesus
In unending glory bright?
Those who bore their cross beside Him,
With the Lamb endured dark night.

Face of Jesus, Light so wondrous,
Shining like the sun so bright,
Son of God, so splendid, precious,
Filling heav'n with beauteous light.

Praise your suff'ring. 'Twill bring blessing,
Heav'nly joys and bliss unknown.
Let us gladly bear our crosses;
They'll bring glory at the throne.

Heav'n is ringing, all are singing
Suff'ring's song before the throne.
There Christ's wounds shine forth, proclaiming
Suff'ring brings us joy unknown.

ACKNOWLEDGEMENTS

Scripture quotations not otherwise identified are taken from the *Revised Standard Version of the Bible*, copyrighted 1946 and 1952, © 1971 and 1973, by the Division of Christian Education of the National Council of the Churches of Christ in the USA, and used by permission.

Scripture quotations identified AV are taken from the King James Version of the Bible.

Scripture quotations identified GNB are taken from the *Good News Bible* — Old Testament: Copyright © American Bible Society 1976, New Testament: Copyright © American Bible Society 1966, 1971, 1976.

Scripture quotation identified AB is taken from *The Amplified Bible*, Old Testament, Copyright © 1962, 1964, Zondervan Publishing House.

Scripture quotation identified LB is taken from *The Living Bible*, © 1971, Tyndale House Publishers.

Scripture quotation identified NEB is taken from *The New English Bible*, copyrighted 1961 and 1970 by the Delegates of the Oxford University Press and the Syndics of the Cambridge University Press.

Most of the devotional songs included in this book have been taken from *My Father, I Trust You* (Songs of Trust and Dedication) by Basilea Schlink.

Other books by Basilea Schlink:

BEHOLD`HIS LOVE

FATHER OF COMFORT (daily readings)

HOPE FOR MAN IN A HOPELESS WORLD

I FOUND THE KEY TO THE HEART OF GOD

A MATTER OF LIFE AND DEATH

MIRROR OF CONSCIENCE (booklet)

MY ALL FOR HIM

PRAYING OUR WAY THROUGH LIFE (booklet)

RULED BY THE SPIRIT

YOU WILL NEVER BE THE SAME